Published by D Publishing Group™ Powered by D Investment Enterprise LLC

THE COVENANT DECLARATION

We enter into this 30-day protocol not just to survive the friction of partnership, but to build a structure that thrives in it. We recognize that a strong relationship is not sustained by temporary feelings; it is built through daily, operational discipline. We agree to lay down our defenses, dismantle our inherited dysfunctions, and forge an unbreakable, trauma-informed union.

Before God and each other, we make the following operational commitments:

- **To Gather Data, Not Defenses:** *I will master the discipline of listening. I will seek to understand your reality before allowing my nervous system to react.*
- **To Neutralize Conflict:** *I will take ownership of my tone, volume, and pacing. I will use them as tactical tools to maintain our emotional safety, even in disagreement.*
- **To Build a Shared Reality:** *I will stop fighting for my individual perspective and start aligning my daily operations with our ultimate spiritual vision.*
- **To Break Generational Patterns:** *I will actively identify the inherited dysfunctions I brought into this union, and I will dismantle them to protect our legacy.*

By signing this document, we establish this covenant as the governing constitution of our relationship. We dedicate our future, our operations, and our lineage to God, asking for the grace to uphold this standard every single day.

Partner 1 Signature: ________________________________ Date:____________

Partner 2 Signature: ________________________________Date:____________

HOW TO USE THIS DEVOTIONAL
Each day includes:
-Scripture
-Reflection
-Discussion Questions
-Couple Exercise
-Prayer Focus

Note: Starting in Section II, a trauma-informed "Clinical Focus" is introduced to assist with emotional regulation during deeper discussions.

Set aside 20–30 minutes nightly. Approach each discussion with humility, emotional regulation, and mutual respect.

Published by D Publishing Group™ Powered by D Investment Enterprise LLC

SECTION I- FOUNDATION
(Days 1–7)

Published by D Publishing Group™ Powered by D Investment Enterprise LLC

DAY 1: Designed, Not Random

Genesis 2:18

> **Reflection**
> Partnership was God's idea. You are not an
> accidental pairing.

Discuss — What attracted us initially? What keeps us aligned now?

Exercise — List three ways you strengthen each other.

Prayer — Thank God for intentional design.

Published by D Publishing Group™ Powered by D Investment Enterprise LLC

Reflections

Clinically Designed ™
OWNED BY MIARAH JONES LLC

DAY 2 -Strength Corresponding

Genesis 2:20–23

> ### Reflection
> "Helper" means strength equal and
> corresponding — not subordinate.

Discuss Where do we complement instead of compete? Where does ego show up?

Exercise Affirm one strength in your partner.

Prayer Pray against comparison and pride.

Published by D Publishing Group™ Powered by D Investment Enterprise LLC

Reflections

DAY 3 - Unity

Genesis 2:24

> **Reflection**
> Leaving and cleaving requires maturity.

Discuss What external influences affect us? How do we protect unity?

Exercise Set one boundary that protects your relationship.

Prayer Protection over your bond.

Published by D Publishing Group™ Powered by D Investment Enterprise LLC

Reflections

DAY 4 - Love Defined

1 Corinthians 13:4–5

> **Reflection**
> Love is behavioral, not merely emotional.

Discuss Where do I need more patience? Do I keep score?

Exercise Apologize for one small habit that disrupts peace.

Prayer Increase patience and humility.

Reflections

DAY 5 - Honor

Romans 12:10

> ### Reflection
> Honor is proactive, not reactive.

Discuss How do we show public respect?

Exercise Send a respectful affirmation to your partner during the day.

Prayer Ask for a heart that naturally honors your spouse.

Published by D Publishing Group™ Powered by D Investment Enterprise LLC

Reflections

DAY 6 - Submission (Mutual)

Ephesians 5:21

Reflection
Mutual submission requires shared
humility.

Discuss Where do I resist yielding?

Exercise Allow your partner to decide something small today.

Prayer Pray for a spirit of mutual yielding.

Published by D Publishing Group™ Powered by D Investment Enterprise LLC

Reflections

Published by D Publishing Group™ Powered by D Investment Enterprise LLC

DAY 7 - Rest & Reflection

Psalm 127:1

Reflection
God builds what lasts.

Exercise Review the week. Celebrate growth.

Prayer Thank God for the foundation being built.

Reflections

SECTION II - COMMUNICATION
(Days 8–14)

Published by D Publishing Group™ Powered by D Investment Enterprise LLC

DAY 8 - The Discipline of Data Gathering

James 1:19

"Everyone should be quick to listen, slow to speak and slow to become angry."

Reflection: Listening is not just waiting for your turn to speak; it is the active discipline of gathering data. When we react quickly, we often respond to our own assumptions rather than our partner's reality.

> ### Clinical Focus: Trauma-Informed
> When the nervous system feels threatened, the brain prioritizes defense over comprehension. Being "quick to listen" requires biological regulation. You cannot effectively hear your partner if you are in a state of hyperarousal (fight or flight).

◆ **Discuss:** What physical signs in my body indicate I have stopped listening and started defending? What tone of voice helps my nervous system feel safe enough to actually hear you?

◆ **Exercise:** Execute a 5-minute uninterrupted listening protocol. Partner A speaks for 2.5 minutes about a current stressor. Partner B only listens, then simply says, "Thank you for sharing that." Switch roles.

◆ **Prayer:** Ask for the discipline to pause, regulate, and truly hear each other before reacting.

Reflections

DAY 9 - Tone as a Regulatory Tool

Proverbs 15:1

"A *gentle answer turns away wrath, but a harsh word stirs up anger.*"

Reflection: The substance of what you say is often lost if the delivery is destructive. A gentle answer is not weakness; it is a tactical choice to de-escalate a volatile situation and maintain structural integrity in the relationship.

Clinical Focus (Co-Regulation):

Human nervous systems constantly scan each other for safety cues (neuroception). A harsh tone signals a threat, instantly triggering your partner's defense mechanisms. A regulated, calm tone acts as an anchor, helping your partner's nervous system down-regulate and return to a state of calm.

◆ **Discuss:** When we disagree, does my tone typically invite safety or signal a threat? How can we gently signal to each other when the volume or tone is escalating too high?

◆ **Exercise:** Practice the "Volume Drop." The next time you feel frustration rising today, intentionally lower your speaking volume by half and slow your cadence. Notice the immediate shift in the room's energy.

◆ **Prayer:** Pray for the awareness to manage your tone, using it to heal rather than to strike.

Published by D Publishing Group™ Powered by D Investment Enterprise LLC

Reflections

DAY 10 - The Psychological Weight of Words

Proverbs 18:21
"The tongue has the power of life and death, and those who love it will eat its fruit."

Reflection: Words are the building blocks of your shared reality. Critical, sarcastic, or dismissive language systematically dismantles trust, while affirming, truthful language reinforces the foundation.

> **Clinical Focus (Verbal Impact):**
> The brain processes emotional pain and physical pain in the same areas. Repeated harsh words create emotional bruising that can lead to a "fawn" or "freeze" trauma response in your partner, causing them to shrink or shut down to avoid further injury.

◆ **Discuss:** What is one phrase or word I use that makes you feel dismissed or minimized? What words of affirmation make you feel most secure?

◆ **Exercise:** For the next 24 hours, implement a "Zero Sarcasm, Zero Criticism" protocol. Replace any critical thought with a request for a specific need.

◆ **Prayer:** Ask God to filter your speech, ensuring your words only breathe life and security into your partner.

Reflections

Published by D Publishing Group™ Powered by D Investment Enterprise LLC

DAY 11 - Safe Confrontation

Ephesians 4:15

"Instead, speaking the truth in love, we will grow to become in every respect the mature body of him who is the head, that is, Christ."

Reflection: Avoiding conflict is not peace; it is simply delayed warfare. Speaking the truth is mandatory for growth, but doing so "in love" means delivering the truth in a way your partner can safely receive it without feeling attacked.

> **Clinical Focus (Radical Candor & Safety):**
> Confrontation without emotional safety triggers defensiveness. A trauma-informed approach to conflict separates the person from the behavior. You are addressing an action, not attacking their identity or worth.

◆**Discuss:** When I bring up a difficult truth, do you feel like I am attacking the problem or attacking you? How can we frame our complaints so they sound like requests for connection rather than indictments?

◆ **Exercise:** Use the "I feel / I need" framework. Practice saying: "When [specific event] happened, I felt [emotion]. In the future, I need [specific action]."

◆ **Prayer:** Pray for the courage to address hard truths, and the profound humility to do so with grace.

Reflections

DAY 12 - Eliminating Contempt

Ephesians 4:29

"Do not let any unwholesome talk come out of your mouths, but only what is helpful for building others up according to their needs, that it may benefit those who listen."

Reflection: Unwholesome talk isn't just profanity; it is any language designed to demean or degrade. Contempt—acting superior or disgusted by your partner—is the single greatest predictor of relational failure.

> **Clinical Focus (Contempt & Erosion):**
> Contempt destroys emotional safety because it communicates, "You are fundamentally flawed and beneath me." It bypasses standard conflict and strikes directly at the core of a person's psychological safety.

◈ **Discuss:** Do either of us struggle with eye-rolling, mocking, or hostile humor during disagreements? How can we build a culture of profound mutual respect, even when we are deeply frustrated?

◈ **Exercise:** Identify one "corrupt" communication habit you personally default to (e.g., interrupting, sighing loudly, using absolutes like "You always..."). Commit to catching yourself and stopping it today.

◈ **Prayer:** Ask God to reveal any hidden contempt in your heart and replace it with unconditional respect.

Reflections

Published by D Publishing Group™ Powered by D Investment Enterprise LLC

DAY 13 - Clearing the Somatic Ledger

Colossians 3:13

"Bear with each other and forgive one another if any of you has a grievance against someone. Forgive as the Lord forgave you."

Reflection: Keeping score is an exhausting way to live. Forgiveness is not about saying the offense didn't hurt; it is about refusing to let past offenses dictate your future operations. It is clearing the ledger so you can move forward.

Clinical Focus (Resentment Tracking):
The body keeps the score. Unforgiveness is chronic stress. Holding onto resentment keeps your nervous system in a low-grade state of hyper-vigilance, preventing true intimacy and physical relaxation with your partner.

◆ **Discuss:** Is there a specific grievance from the past that I am still privately holding against you? What do I need from you—or from myself—to finally close that account and release it?

◆ **Exercise:** The "Ledger Clear." Look at each other and specifically name one small thing you are choosing to forgive and let go of today. Say aloud, "I release this, and I am no longer holding it against you."

◆ **Prayer:** Pray for the strength to forgive completely, breaking the cycle of resentment.

Reflections

DAY 14 - The Protocol of Peace

Romans 12:18
"If it is possible, as far as it depends on you, live at peace with everyone."

Reflection: You cannot control your partner's reactions, but you are 100% responsible for your own operations. Choosing peace often means surrendering the ego's intense desire to be "right" or to have the last word.

Clinical Focus (Ego vs. Connection):
In moments of conflict, you are often forced to choose between winning the argument or protecting the connection. A trauma-informed partner recognizes that "winning" at the expense of their partner's emotional safety is actually a structural loss for the relationship.

◆**Discuss:** In our recent disagreements, have I prioritized being right over being connected? What does "living at peace" actively look like for us in our home?

◆**Exercise:** The De-escalation Agreement. Agree right now that either of you can call a "Peace Pause" when an argument is looping without resolution. You agree to stop, separate for 20 minutes to regulate, and return calmly.

◆**Prayer:** Ask God to make your relationship a sanctuary of peace, insulated from the chaos of the outside world.

Reflections

Published by D Publishing Group™ Powered by D Investment Enterprise LLC

SECTION III - DISCIPLINE
(Days 15–21)

Published by D Publishing Group™ Powered by D Investment Enterprise LLC

DAY 15 - The Architecture of Self-Control

Galatians 5:22-23

"But the fruit of the Spirit is love, joy, peace, forbearance, kindness, goodness, faithfulness, gentleness and self-control."

Reflection: Self-control isn't just willpower; it is the operational discipline to not let temporary emotions dictate permanent actions. It is the internal braking system that prevents you from crashing the relationship during a heated moment.

> **Clinical Focus (Nervous System Regulation):** A dysregulated nervous system cannot access the prefrontal cortex (the brain's logic and impulse-control center). True self-control begins with physiological soothing—recognizing biological activation before it becomes a verbal reaction.

◆**Discuss:** What is my personal physical "tell" (e.g., clenched jaw, racing heart, rapid speech) when I am losing emotional regulation? How can we help each other recognize these signs before a conversation spirals?

◆**Exercise:** Practice a 60-second synchronized breathing protocol together. Inhale for 4 seconds, exhale for 6 seconds. Doing this physically lowers heart rates and proves you can regain control of your biology on command.

◆**Prayer:** Ask for the discipline to master your own impulses rather than trying to control your partner.

Reflections

DAY 16 - Micro-Stewardship and Trust

Luke 16:10

"Whoever can be trusted with very little can also be trusted with much."

Reflection: Trust is not built in massive, sweeping gestures. It is built in the microscopic management of daily promises. How you handle the small, seemingly insignificant details of your shared life predicts your capacity to handle major crises.

Clinical Focus (Predictability & Safety):
The human brain craves predictability to feel secure. When a partner consistently follows through on small commitments, it signals to the other's nervous system that the environment is safe. Unpredictability breeds chronic relational anxiety.

◈**Discuss:** What small, daily action makes you feel the most secure in my reliability? In what minor areas have I let the ball drop, unintentionally creating inconsistency?

◈**Exercise:** Commit to completing one micro-task today exactly when you said you would, without being reminded or seeking praise for it.

◈**Prayer:** Pray for the integrity to be an excellent steward of your partner's trust in the small things.

Reflections

Published by D Publishing Group™ Powered by D Investment Enterprise LLC

DAY 17 - Boundary Defenses for the Mind

Proverbs 4:23

"Above all else, guard your heart, for everything you do flows from it."

Reflection: Your mind is the control room of your relationship. Whatever you allow to influence your thoughts—whether it is social media, cynical friends, or past baggage—will eventually dictate your behavior toward your partner.

> **Clinical Focus (Cognitive Distortions):** Unchecked assumptions lead to internal "storytelling." When we assume negative intent from our partner without verifying the facts, our brain reacts to the manufactured story as if it were a literal threat, bypassing reality entirely.

◈**Discuss:** What outside influences most negatively affect how I view our relationship or myself? Do I tend to assume the best or the worst about your intentions when you make a mistake?

◈**Exercise:** Identify one negative assumption you've made about your partner recently. Fact-check it with them out loud today by asking, "The story I am telling myself right now is [X]... is that accurate?"

◈**Prayer:** Ask God to filter your influences and protect your mind from narratives that divide your partnership.

Reflections

DAY 18 - The Operations of Mutual Service

Colossians 3:23

"Whatever you do, work at it with all your heart, as working for the Lord, not for human masters."

Reflection: Serving your partner is not a transaction; it is an investment into the structural health of the relationship. When both partners operate with a mindset of mutual service, no one feels used, and everyone feels valued.

> **Clinical Focus (Reciprocity vs. Scorekeeping):** Secure attachment relies on natural, unforced reciprocity. Scorekeeping creates a transactional environment where love feels conditional. This triggers anxiety, resentment, and a fear of "not doing enough to earn my keep."

Discuss: When do I feel most served and valued by you? Be honest: Do I have a tendency to keep score of who does more around the house or in the relationship?

Exercise: Perform one unseen act of service for your partner today without announcing it, complaining about it, or expecting acknowledgment.

Prayer: Pray for a servant's heart that gives freely without demanding an immediate return on investment.

Reflections

Clinically Designed™

OWNED BY MIARAH JONES LLC

DAY 19 - The Ego Audit

Philippians 2:3
"Do nothing out of selfish ambition or vain conceit. Rather, in humility value others above yourselves."

Reflection: Pride is the ultimate structural flaw in a relationship. It makes you rigid and unable to adapt. Humility is the willingness to submit your ego for the sake of the union. It is the strength to say, "I was wrong."

Clinical Focus (Defensiveness & Vulnerability): Defensiveness is a shield the ego uses to avoid the vulnerability of being wrong. In a trauma-aware framework, dismantling defensiveness requires creating an environment where making a mistake does not equal being a bad person.

Discuss: In what specific area of our relationship is my pride currently preventing us from growing? What makes it difficult for me to admit when I am wrong?

Exercise: Look at your partner today and say out loud, "I am willing to be wrong in order to make us right."

Prayer: Ask God to break down your ego and replace it with a relentless pursuit of unity.

Reflections

____

____

____

____

____

____

____

____

____

____

____

____

____

____

____

____

____

____

____

____

____

____

____

____

Published by D Publishing Group™ Powered by D Investment Enterprise LLC

DAY 20 - Containment Protocols for Conflict

Matthew 18:15

"If your brother or sister sins, go and point out their fault, just between the two of you."

Reflection: Conflict should never be a spectator sport. Airing grievances publicly, venting on social media, or complaining to family members breaches the protective walls of your partnership.

> **Clinical Focus (Triangulation):**
> Pulling a third party into a two-person conflict is called triangulation. It is highly toxic, dilutes trust, and creates an unsafe, unstable relational dynamic. Safety requires that the dyad (the two of you) remains a closed, secure loop.

◈ **Discuss:** Have we established clear boundaries about what stays strictly private between us? Who are the safe, objective people (like a therapist or mentor) we are allowed to consult when we are stuck?

◈ **Exercise:** Establish a strict "No Venting" policy. Agree right now that you will not speak negatively about each other to friends or family as a way to relieve personal frustration.

◈ **Prayer:** Pray for the wisdom to keep your conflicts contained and to protect your partner's reputation at all costs.

Reflections

Published by D Publishing Group™ Powered by D Investment Enterprise LLC

DAY 21 - The Yield of Discomfort

Hebrews 12:11
"No discipline seems pleasant at the time, but painful. Later on, however, it produces a harvest of righteousness and peace for those who have been trained by it."

Reflection: Growth is inherently uncomfortable. Avoiding hard conversations or necessary behavioral changes keeps the relationship stagnant. Leaning into the discomfort is the price you pay for long-term peace.

Clinical Focus (The Window of Tolerance): Relational growth only happens at the very edges of your emotional "window of tolerance." Avoiding discomfort shrinks this window, making the relationship fragile. Safely leaning into difficult emotional work expands your capacity to handle stress as a team.

◆**Discuss:** What uncomfortable conversation or habit change have we been avoiding because it feels too heavy? How can we support each other through the friction of changing old patterns?

◆**Exercise:** Schedule a 15-minute block this week to tackle one uncomfortable topic you've been avoiding, using the listening and regulation tools you've practiced over the last 20 days.

◆**Prayer:** Thank God for the friction that refines you, and ask for the endurance to see the discipline through.

Reflections

Clinically Designed™

OWNED BY MIARAH JONES LLC

Published by D Publishing Group™ Powered by D Investment Enterprise LLC

SECTION IV - VISION
(Days 22–30)

Published by D Publishing Group™ Powered by D Investment Enterprise LLC

DAY 22 - The Architecture of Shared Reality

Habakkuk 2:2

"Write down the revelation and make it plain on tablets so that a herald may run with it."

Reflection: A vision cannot be executed if it only exists in one person's head. Writing down your shared goals is an operational necessity. It aligns your daily operations and ensures both partners are running toward the exact same finish line.

Clinical Focus (Shared Meaning):
Relational distress often stems from couples living in two different psychological realities. Creating a shared vision anchors both nervous systems in a common purpose. When the brain knows where the relationship is going, it requires less energy to constantly scan the horizon for threats.

Discuss: What is one long-term goal we are actively building toward right now? Do our daily habits actually reflect the future we say we want to build?

Exercise: The Vision Protocol. Take 10 minutes tonight to write down three specific, measurable goals for your relationship over the next 12 months (e.g., financial, spiritual, or relational).

Prayer: Pray for absolute clarity and structural alignment in your shared future.

Published by D Publishing Group™ Powered by D Investment Enterprise LLC

Reflections

DAY 23 -Executive Functioning vs. Impulse

Proverbs 24:3

"By wisdom a house is built, and through understanding it is established."

Reflection: You do not build a lasting legacy on temporary feelings. A strong relationship requires the discipline to make decisions based on structural wisdom rather than emotional impulse.

> **Clinical Focus (The Prefrontal Cortex):**
> Impulsive decisions—whether financial or relational—are driven by the amygdala (the emotional center). Building a "house" requires engaging the prefrontal cortex, which governs logic, planning, and delayed gratification. Wisdom is the psychological ability to pause the impulse and consult the blueprint.

◆**Discuss:** In what area of our life do we tend to operate on impulse rather than planning? How can we structurally support each other when making high-stakes decisions?

◆**Exercise:** Implement a "24-Hour Hold" rule. Agree that any major decision (financial purchase, schedule commitment, etc.) requires a 24-hour cooling-off period before either of you say yes.

◆**Prayer:** Ask God to establish your household on a foundation of sound, disciplined wisdom.

Reflections

Published by D Publishing Group™ Powered by D Investment Enterprise LLC

DAY 24 - Alignment of Core Values

Matthew 6:33

"But seek first his kingdom and his righteousness, and all these things will be given to you as well."

Reflection: If the order of operations is wrong, the equation fails. Seeking spiritual alignment first is not just religious advice; it is the ultimate stabilizing force. When your highest priorities are aligned, the secondary issues naturally fall into place.

> **Clinical Focus (Cognitive Dissonance):**
> When a couple's daily behaviors contradict their stated core values, it creates cognitive dissonance—a low-grade, chronic mental stress. Aligning your schedule and your finances with your spiritual values eliminates this internal friction.

Discuss: Look at our calendar and our bank account. Do they reflect the values we claim are most important? What is one distraction we need to eliminate to properly order our priorities?

Exercise: The Value Audit. Identify one area where your time or resources are leaking toward something that does not serve your ultimate vision. Agree to cut it this week.

Prayer: Pray for the discipline to keep the main thing the main thing, seeking God's blueprint above cultural pressure.

Reflections

Published by D Publishing Group™ Powered by D Investment Enterprise LLC

DAY 25 - Breaking the Generational Chain

Psalm 78:4

"We will not hide them from their descendants; we will tell the next generation the praiseworthy deeds of the Lord."

Reflection: You are either passing down a legacy or passing down a liability. Generational thinking requires you to look beyond your own comfort and ask: What patterns are we establishing that our children will have to inherit?

Clinical Focus (Intergenerational Trauma): Trauma, coping mechanisms, and communication styles are passed down through families both biologically and behaviorally. A trauma-informed partnership actively identifies toxic family-of-origin patterns and consciously decides: "This stops with us."

Discuss: What is one unhealthy relational habit we inherited from our families that we refuse to pass on? What is one new, healthy protocol we are intentionally starting in this generation?

Exercise: Verbally declare a "Pattern Break." Look at each other and name one specific dysfunction you are locking out of your relationship permanently.

Prayer: Ask God for the strength to be the generation that breaks the curse and establishes the blessing.

Reflections

Published by D Publishing Group™ Powered by D Investment Enterprise LLC

DAY 26 - The Secure Base in Adversity

Joshua 1:9

"Have I not commanded you? Be strong and courageous. Do not be afraid; do not be discouraged, for the Lord your God will be with you wherever you go."

Reflection: Courage is not the absence of fear; it is the execution of duty despite the fear. When the outside world introduces volatility, your partnership must be the impenetrable fortress you retreat to for reinforcement.

Clinical Focus (The Secure Base):
In attachment theory, a "secure base" is a relationship safe enough that it allows an individual to confidently explore the world and take risks. When your partner knows you have their back entirely, their capacity to handle external stress multiplies exponentially.

◆**Discuss:** Do I act as a secure base for you when you are facing heavy stress at work or in life? How can I better stand shoulder-to-shoulder with you when we face external threats?

◆**Exercise:** Look your partner in the eye and say: "No matter what volatility we face outside these walls, I am your ally, and we face it as a united front."

◆**Prayer:** Pray for unwavering courage and a bond that tightens under pressure.

Reflections

Published by D Publishing Group™ Powered by D Investment Enterprise LLC

DAY 27 - The Neuroplasticity of Gratitude

1 Thessalonians 5:18
"Give thanks in all circumstances; for this is God's will for you in Christ Jesus."

Reflection: Gratitude is a defensive perimeter against bitterness. It is impossible to hold deep contempt and profound gratitude for someone at the exact same time. Cultivating gratitude is a deliberate, daily operational choice.

Clinical Focus (Rewiring the Brain):
The human brain has a "negativity bias"—it naturally scans for what is wrong to protect you from danger. Practicing intentional gratitude physically rewires the brain's neural pathways (neuroplasticity), forcing it to recognize safety, value, and connection in your partner.

◆**Discuss:** Have I been focusing more on your deficits or your assets lately? What is one specific thing you did this week that I did not properly thank you for?

◆**Exercise:** The Asset Focus. Name three highly specific things you deeply appreciate about your partner's character (not just things they do for you, but who they are).

◆**Prayer:** Ask God to override your negativity bias and give you eyes to see the immense value in your partner.

Published by D Publishing Group™ Powered by D Investment Enterprise LLC

Reflections

Published by D Publishing Group™ Powered by D Investment Enterprise LLC

DAY 28 - The Forge of Volatility

James 1:2–4
"Consider it pure joy, my brothers and sisters, whenever you face trials of many kinds, because you know that the testing of your faith produces perseverance."

Reflection: Hard seasons are not evidence that the relationship is failing; they are the forge where the relationship is hardened. A partnership that has never been tested is fragile. Surviving the fire together produces an unbreakable structural integrity.

Clinical Focus (Post-Traumatic Growth):
While trauma and severe stress can fracture a relationship, navigating it successfully as a team leads to "post-traumatic growth." The dyad emerges with a deeper level of empathy, a higher threshold for stress, and absolute proof of their resilience.

Discuss: What is the hardest season we have survived together, and how did it make us stronger? How do we prevent turning on each other when the pressure is high?

Exercise: Acknowledge your track record. Remind each other of a past crisis you successfully navigated and celebrate the resilience you built from it.

Prayer: Thank God for the friction that has refined your relationship and the trials that have proven your bond.

Published by D Publishing Group™ Powered by D Investment Enterprise LLC

Reflections

Published by D Publishing Group™ Powered by D Investment Enterprise LLC

DAY 29 - The Closed System

Ecclesiastes 4:9–12

"Two are better than one... A cord of three strands is not quickly broken."

Reflection: A strong relationship is a closed system. God is the anchor, and the two of you are the structure. Letting outside interference, opinions, or divided loyalties into the system weakens the cord and compromises the integrity of the whole unit.

> **Clinical Focus (Boundary Fortification):**
> A secure attachment requires definitive borders. When a couple establishes that their unit is the primary loyalty—above parents, friends, and careers—it signals ultimate safety to the nervous system. The threat of abandonment is neutralized.

◆**Discuss:** Are there any "leaks" in our system right now where outside influences are causing internal division? How do we actively protect the third strand (our spiritual foundation) in our daily lives?

◆**Exercise:** Draft a one-sentence "Boundary Protocol" that defines how you will protect your relationship from outside interference moving forward.

◆**Prayer:** Pray for a fortified relationship, sealed against division and anchored completely in faith.

Reflections

Published by D Publishing Group™ Powered by D Investment Enterprise LLC

DAY 30 - The Covenant Execution

Ruth 1:16

"Where you go I will go, and where you stay I will stay. Your people will be my people and your God my God."

Reflection: Commitment is not a feeling; it is an executed contract. A covenant means that the exit doors are locked. When leaving is no longer an option, you are forced to do the hard work of building, repairing, and growing together.

> **Clinical Focus (Rituals of Connection):**
> The nervous system thrives on permanence. Formalizing your commitment through spoken declarations and written covenants serves as a profound "ritual of connection," deeply embedding a sense of psychological safety and permanent belonging into the brain.

Discuss: What has been the most valuable realization for you over these last 30 days? What is our next operational step to ensure we do not lose this momentum?

Exercise: The Final Declaration. Read the Final Covenant Page (from the intro) aloud to each other. Sign it, date it, and establish it as the governing document of your relationship.

Prayer: Dedicate your future, your operations, and your legacy to God, asking for the grace to uphold this covenant every single day.

Published by D Publishing Group™ Powered by D Investment Enterprise LLC

Reflections

APPENDIX:
References & Recommended Clinical Reading

1. **Neurobiology & Somatic Regulation**
   a. **Perry, Bruce D., MD, PhD, & Winfrey, Oprah**. What Happened to You? Conversations on Trauma, Resilience, and Healing. (Foundational reading for the Neurosequential Model of Therapeutics and understanding how the brainstem processes threat before the cortex can process logic).
   b. **van der Kolk, Bessel, MD.** The Body Keeps the Score: Brain, Mind, and Body in the Healing of Trauma. (The definitive text on how trauma alters the physical architecture of the body and nervous system).
2. **Emotional Regulation & Distress Tolerance**
   a. **Linehan, Marsha M., PhD, ABPP.** DBT Skills Training Manual. (The creator of Dialectical Behavior Therapy. The distress tolerance and emotional regulation concepts adapted in this devotional are rooted in her foundational architecture).
3. **Generational & Inherited Trauma**
   a. **Wolynn, Mark.** It Didn't Start with You: How Inherited Family Trauma Shapes Who We Are and How to End the Cycle. (Essential reading for understanding the biological and psychological mechanisms of passing down, and breaking, generational cycles).
4. **Relational Architecture & Conflict De-escalation**
   a. **Gottman, John M., PhD, & Silver, Nan.** The Seven Principles for Making Marriage Work. (The industry standard for data-driven couples therapy, conflict neutralization, and building shared reality).

All proprietary psychological modalities, including DBT and NMT, remain the intellectual property of their respective creators. This devotional serves as an educational and spiritual integration tool and does not replace licensed mental health or medical services.

Published by D Publishing Group™ Powered by D Investment Enterprise LLC